PLAN

by Sharon Fear

illustrated by Phillip Dvorak

MODERN CURRICULUM PRESS

Pearson Learning Group

Tap. Tap. Tap.
Was there a thing in the apartment?

"Come on, dog," said Jack.
"Now sleep close to me."

Tick. Tick. Tick.
Was there a BIG thing in the apartment?
Could it be an elephant?

"Come on, cat," said Jack.
"Now sleep close to me."

Bump. Ping! Plink!
"That is too much!" said Jack.
"Now it sounds like pianos playing.
Dog, cat, I have a plan."

"MEOW!" yelled the cat.
"RUFF! RUFF!" yelled the dog.
"BE QUIET! NOW YOU NEED TO GO TO SLEEP!" yelled Jack.
"That is the plan."

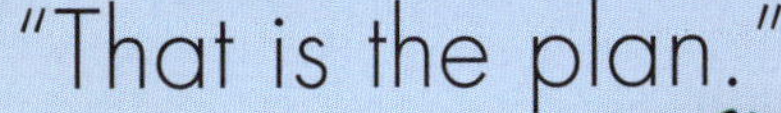

And that is what they did.